D1029979

OUTLAWS, GUNSLINGERS, AND THIEVES

HEATHER E. SCHWARTZ

Lerner Publications Company • Minneapolis

To my boys, Philip, Nolan, and Griffin —HES

Lerner Publications Company
A division of Lerner Publishing Group, Inc.
241 First Avenue North
Minneapolis, MN 55401 U.S.A.

Website address: www.lernerbooks.com

Library of Congress Cataloging-in-Publication Data

Schwartz, Heather E.
    Outlaws, gunslingers, and thieves / by Heather E. Schwartz.
      p. cm. — (ShockZone™—Villains)
    Includes index.
    ISBN 978–1–4677–0605–6 (lib. bdg. : alk. paper)
    1. Outlaws—West (U.S.)—History—19th century—Juvenile literature. 2. Frontier
and pioneer life—West (U.S.)—Juvenile literature. 3. West (U.S.)—History—19th
century—Juvenile literature. I. Title.
F596.S345 2013
978'.02—dc23   2012019113

Manufactured in the United States of America
1 – PC – 12/31/12

TABLE OF CONTENTS

If you're reading this book—and obviously, you are—you clearly weren't alive during the 1800s. Still, **you can probably describe a western outlaw, right?** Murderous tough guy. Gets into fights. Robs banks, fleeing the scene on horseback just ahead of the law.

But what about those who did things a little...differently? You know, outlaws who chopped up their victims' bodies. Wrote poetry to leave at the scene of a crime. Dressed in clothes more suited to a proper lady than a dangerous cowgirl.

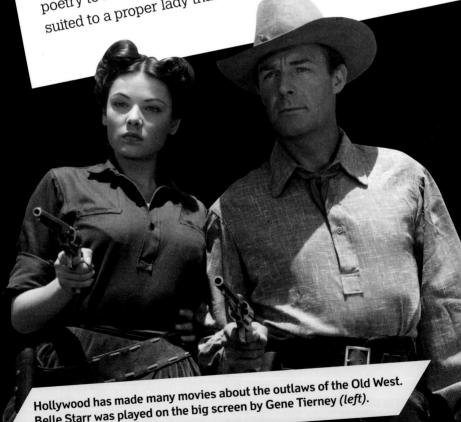

Hollywood has made many movies about the outlaws of the Old West. Belle Starr was played on the big screen by Gene Tierney *(left)*.

Outlaws of the Wild West were men *and* women. They committed both typical and not-so-typical crimes. Many of them thought they had perfectly good reasons to commit those crimes. And sometimes, those on the *right* side of the law acted even more crazily than the criminals they were after.

Want to find out who did what—and got away with it? Read on to learn more about the wildest outlaws of the West.

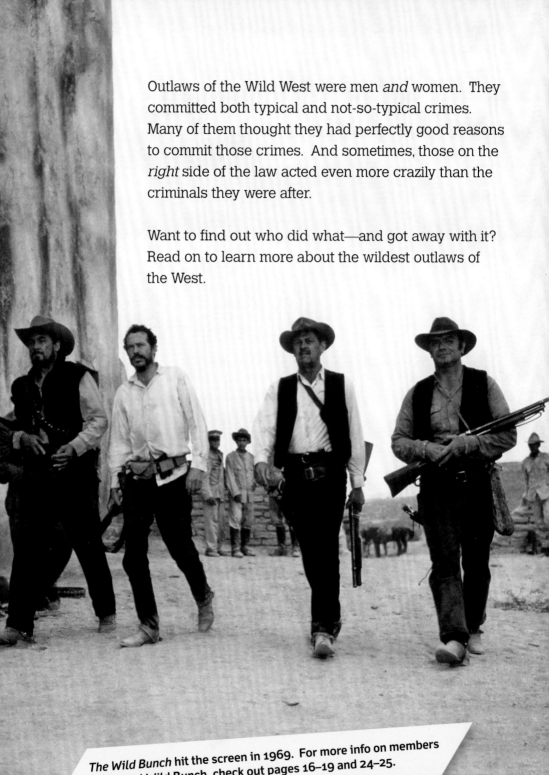

The Wild Bunch hit the screen in 1969. For more info on members of the real Wild Bunch, check out pages 16–19 and 24–25.

JESSE JAMES:
ROBIN HOOD IN DISGUISE?

In the late 1800s, a lot of people thought Jesse James was like Robin Hood, robbing from the rich to give to the poor. But this dude was no kindhearted criminal. He attacked innocent people. When he nabbed loot, he didn't share it. His real goals? Murder, power, and wealth.

Jesse was fourteen when he started training to kill people. During the Civil War (1861–1865), he joined a group of outlaws. Their mission was to terrorize Union (Northern) soldiers in some really nasty ways. The group bashed in skulls, chopped off heads, slashed throats, and tortured people. Then they sliced "trophies" off their victims' bodies—meaning noses, scalps, and other fleshy parts. Ears were especially popular prizes. The outlaws strung them together into gory necklaces.

PISTOL POWER

Jesse James's favorite weapon was the revolver (*at left*, his last gun), a new kind of pistol in the 1800s. Using a revolver, Jesse could fire many bullets in a row without reloading.

After the war, Jesse set out with his brother, Frank. They led a gang robbing banks and trains. On one robbery, the gang went after the Union supporter who had killed the leader of Jesse's old group. They got the wrong guy. But their vicious attempt impressed a newspaper editor and ex-Confederate (Southern) soldier named John Newman Edwards.

Edwards started writing about the James brothers. He made Jesse sound like a hero. Edwards thought Jesse had a right to be angry after losing the war.

Edwards's articles created a myth of Jesse as a Wild West hero. The real truth? Jesse was a cold-blooded killer. He never even made it to the West. He robbed, murdered, and mutilated victims in Missouri, Iowa, Kentucky, and Minnesota.

mutilate = to disfigure someone, often by cutting off a body part

Union soldiers wanted to avoid run-ins with Jesse and his gang of outlaws.

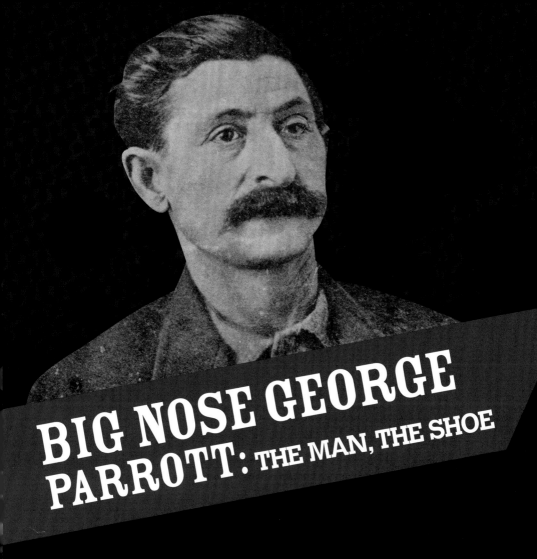

BIG NOSE GEORGE PARROTT: THE MAN, THE SHOE

Will the real outlaw please stand up? In the case of Big Nose George Parrott, it's not so simple to tell the bad guys from the good guys. Alive, George was just your ordinary thief and murderer who dismembered his victims. Dead, he was a pair of shoes. Here's how it all went down.

Working with a gang, George tried to rob a train in Wyoming in 1878. When lawmen showed up, the gang killed and dismembered them. Afterward, George left the state. But he wasn't too smart about hiding out. One day, he got drunk in a bar and started bragging about his crimes. Surprise, surprise, he was caught and sentenced to hang.

> **dismember =** to cut the limbs, such as the arms and legs, off a body

Once George landed in jail, he unsuccessfully tried to escape. Townspeople stormed the jail. They hanged the outlaw on the spot. Unfortunately, they weren't very good at it. The hanging took more than one try. In the process, George struggled so hard he tore his ears off.

George was finally dead, but his situation was about to get even worse. When his corpse was dangling, along came Dr. Thomas Magee and Dr. John Osborne for the body. Dr. Magee sawed open George's skull. He wanted a look at the criminal's brain. Dr. Osborne went a bit further. He removed skin from George's body. He sent it away to be turned into a pair of shoes. Rumor has it Dr. Osborne wore those shoes for years.

Now *who's* the creepiest character in this story again?

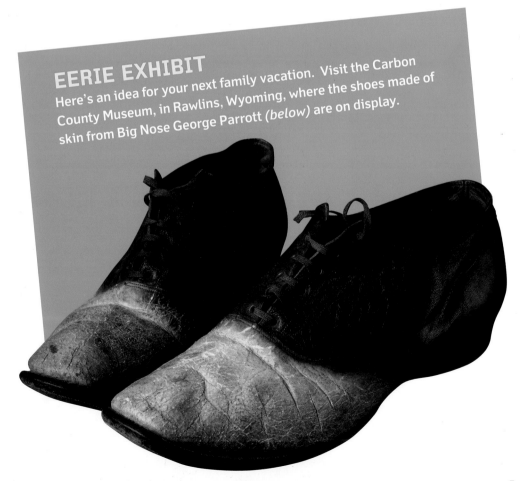

EERIE EXHIBIT
Here's an idea for your next family vacation. Visit the Carbon County Museum, in Rawlins, Wyoming, where the shoes made of skin from Big Nose George Parrott (*below*) are on display.

CHARLES E. BOLLES:
BLACK BART, THE GENTLEMAN THIEF

For most of his life, Charles E. Bolles was an honest man. He worked in California gold mines. He married and had kids. He fought in the Civil War. Ho-hum. After the war, he left home again to work a mine on his own. That's when things went wrong for Charles. Something happened to turn him against Wells Fargo, a banking company. It must have been pretty bad. Charles stopped writing to his wife, leading her to think he had died. It took years before she learned that, instead, he'd turned criminal. His prime target? Wells Fargo, of course.

In his new life of crime, Charles took on a new name: Black Bart.

He robbed almost thirty Wells Fargo stagecoaches. But he took a strangely polite approach. He always said, "Please" when requesting the loot. He disguised his face with a flour sack (with holes cut out for his eyes), but he still placed his hat on his head. And though he carried a gun, he wasn't a killer. He never left dead bodies behind after a robbery. But he did sometimes leave verses of poetry.

When the law tracked him down, Black Bart was charged for just one robbery. His prison time was cut from six years to four years. Crime doesn't pay, but it seems proper behavior just might—even when a guy's clearly an outlaw.

Guards transported money or gold across the country on Wells Fargo Express wagons in the late 1800s.

I rob the rich to feed the poor
Which chardly is a sin,
A widow ne'er knocked at my door
But what I let her in,
So blame me not for what I've done
I don't deserve your curses
And if for any cause I'm hung
Let it be for my verses

Black Bart
The po8

A VILLAIN'S VERSE
Black Bart left this poem at the scene after robbing a stagecoach in 1878:

Here I lay me down to sleep
To wait the coming morrow,
Perhaps success, perhaps defeat,
And everlasting sorrow.
Let come what will I'll try it on,
My condition can't be worse;
And if there's money in that box
Tis munny in my purse!

Another of Black Bart's rhymes ends, "And if for any cause I'm hung Let it be for my verses."

JOAQUIN MURRIETA:
BATMAN'S INSPIRATION

As a Mexican in California around 1850, Joaquin had plenty of reasons to be ticked off. Mexicans battled prejudice and abuse all the time. Some say Joaquin's wife was killed by American gold miners. Some say Joaquin himself was punished for crimes he didn't commit.

Other reports suggest Joaquin wanted justice for Mexico. California had been Mexican territory until 1848. That year Mexico gave California to the United States as part of a treaty (peace agreement). The U.S. government then announced that the land contained gold. It was news to Mexico but not to the U.S. leaders who had signed the treaty.

Whatever the case, Joaquin focused his anger for one purpose: revenge. He became a murderer and a thief. His terror spree in California didn't go unnoticed by lawmen. The call went out. Joaquin was wanted, dead or alive.

The masked avenger Zorro (played by Antonio Banderas in 2005's *The Legend of Zorro*) is supposedly based on the life of Joaquin.

OK, so Joaquin had to be stopped. But did lawmen really have to shoot him, chop off his head, and pickle it in whiskey to prove he was dead? The sheriff took Murrieta's head on tour, with folks paying a dollar for a peek. When the tour ended, the head was displayed at the San Francisco Museum. (It was later destroyed in an earthquake.)

Regardless of Joaquin's grisly end, nothing could stop his legend from living on. To many, this outlaw is a hero for standing up against prejudice. Historians say Joaquin is the inspiration behind at least two heroic figures: Zorro, the fictional masked avenger, and Batman, the comic-book crime fighter.

BELLE STARR:

THE BANDIT QUEEN

Did Belle Starr really dress as a man to help out with robberies? Did she burn down stores? Lead a gang that stole livestock? Hide outlaws on her property? So the story goes, at least according to some historians. Others say she was a fine lady who just happened to have a lot of connections to criminal men.

Belle grew up rich. As part of respectable southern society, she was schooled in music, Greek, and Latin. Of course, she also learned—from her big brother—how to ride and shoot. Those skills would come in handy later.

When the Civil War started, her family went broke. They left their home in Missouri for Texas, looking for a fresh start. But Belle soon lost interest in "respectable" society. Instead, she got friendly with all sorts of outlaws. It all began when her first husband, Jim Reed, started hanging out with the criminal Tom Starr. Tom introduced Jim to a world of murder and thievery. Not all historians are convinced Belle got in on the fun. But her ties with these men earned her a nickname: the Bandit Queen.

Criminal or not, Belle did spend time in jail for stealing horses. Her death also points to some shady behavior. A woman with enemies, she died of two shotgun blasts to the back. Who did it? One of her kids? An outlaw she'd threatened? Several suspects were named, but Belle's murderer was never found.

Belle married Sam Starr, Tom Starr's son, after Jim Reed died. This wanted poster was issued by the U.S. government around 1880.

REWARD

☞ **$10,000** ☜
IN GOLD COIN

Will be paid by the U. S. Government
for the apprehension

DEAD OR ALIVE

of

SAM and BELLE STARR

*Wanted for Robbery, Murder, Treason
and other acts against the peace
and dignity of the U. S.*

THOMAS CRAIL

Major, 8th Missouri Cavalry, Commanding

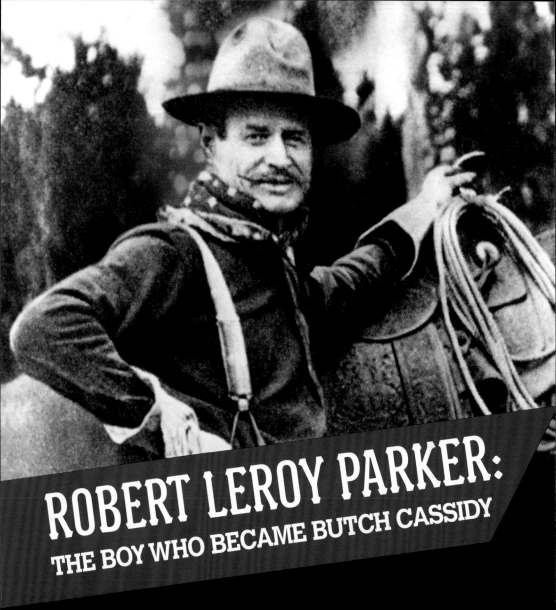

ROBERT LEROY PARKER:
THE BOY WHO BECAME BUTCH CASSIDY

When Robert Leroy Parker was growing up, he was the oldest of thirteen kids in a religious home. That's a nice solid beginning, but who could resist the criminal life with Mike Cassidy living nearby? Hanging with his neighbor, Robert learned about a new way to live. By eighteen, he was on his own—a drifter.

For his first big crime, Robert robbed a bank in Telluride, Colorado. Afterward, he hid from the law by working for a butcher. It was around then that he got creative with his name. Combining his mentor's last name with his new job, Robert created his famous nickname: Butch Cassidy.

As Butch, he grew into his tough-guy role. Butch Cassidy stole horses and spent time in jail. He started a gang called the Wild Bunch. They robbed trains, went wild on vacations, and generally had a grand old time. Until the law interfered, that is.

When detectives came after the Wild Bunch, Butch left for South America with his friend the Sundance Kid and the Kid's girlfriend, Etta Place. They ran a ranch together for a while. But living lawfully wasn't for them. Soon enough, Butch and the Kid were back to their old ways. When the law caught up to them, in 1908, a shootout with Bolivian soldiers left both men dead.

PINKERTON'S IN PURSUIT

Butch Cassidy left the United States when Pinkerton's National Detective Agency went after the Wild Bunch in a big way. The company was famous for foiling a plot to kill Abraham Lincoln in 1861.

Or did it? Some say Butch Cassidy lived on under a new name. In that version of his story, he came back to the United States, ran a business, and died at an old age in a nursing home.

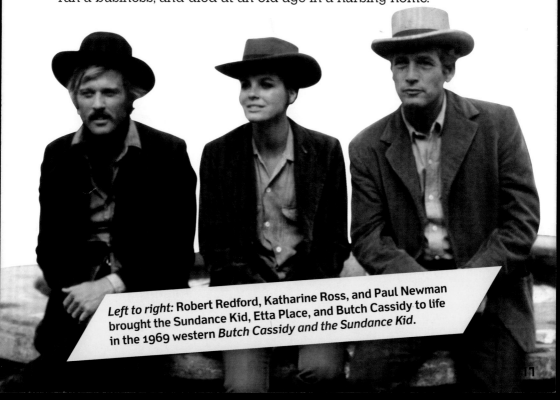

Left to right: Robert Redford, Katharine Ross, and Paul Newman brought the Sundance Kid, Etta Place, and Butch Cassidy to life in the 1969 western *Butch Cassidy and the Sundance Kid.*

HARRY LONGABAUGH:
THE SUNDANCE KID

Harry Longabaugh went to prison just once, for stealing a horse. But that was enough for him to start creating his legend. He was held in the town of Sundance, Wyoming. When he got out, he called himself the Sundance Kid. He headed to the Hole in the Wall, a remote Wyoming spot where outlaws hid. This high area of land was hard to reach and easy to defend. It was there the Sundance Kid started living his legendary life.

When the Sundance Kid met the outlaw Butch Cassidy, he found a friend with similar goals. He joined Cassidy's gang, the Wild Bunch. He earned a reputation for having the fastest shooting skills in the gang. The Wild Bunch held up some trains together but soon had the law on their trail.

In 1901 the Sundance Kid, his girlfriend, Etta Place, and his friend Butch Cassidy left the Wild West for South America. For a while, they tried farming. When that got old, they robbed trains and banks. But leave it to the law to spoil their fun. Eventually, the Sundance Kid and Butch Cassidy were caught in that fateful gun battle with Bolivian soldiers.

GRAVE DIGGER

In 2008 the remains of a man named William Henry Long were dug up. He had died in 1936, and some people thought he was the Sundance Kid, under a different name. Tests couldn't prove that theory. But at least one of his relatives thinks it's true.

Was the Sundance Kid killed? No one's really sure. From that point, he disappeared. Some say he went to his grave. Others believe he got away with his crimes, returning to the United States to live an honest life for the rest of his days.

Robert Redford (who famously played the Sundance Kid in 1969) rides through the area near the Hole in the Wall hideout in Wyoming.

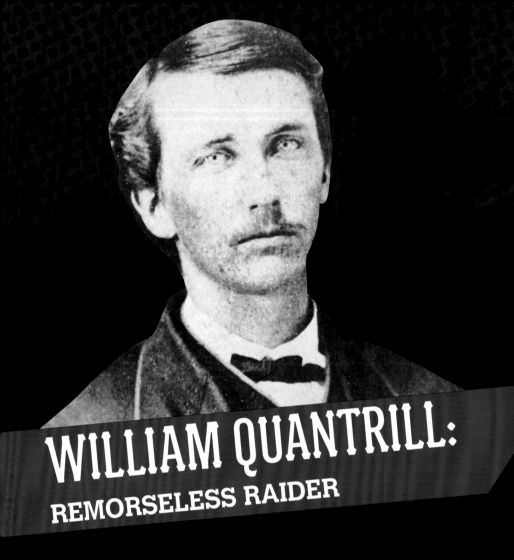

WILLIAM QUANTRILL:
REMORSELESS RAIDER

When William Quantrill joined the Confederate forces during the Civil War, he was already wanted as a murderer and horse thief. Soon he would be feared as a terrorist. William led a savage group for the Confederacy dubbed Quantrill's Raiders. Their job was harassing Union soldiers—and anyone else who took the Union's side.

In August 1863, Quantrill led 450 raiders to an unlucky senator's house in Lawrence, Kansas. You can probably guess that this senator happened to be pro-Union, and Quantrill was after him. While the senator escaped, not everyone in Lawrence was so lucky. Quantrill and his men went on a killing spree. They dragged men and boys out of their houses. They shot them while their families

This engraving of the 1863 attack shows Quantrill's Raiders attacking Lawrence, Kansas.

watched. When the raiders were done, more than 180 men and boys were dead. Just to be extra cruel, the raiders set the city on fire too.

From there, Quantrill's group went on to kill eighty Union soldiers in the Baxter Springs Massacre. Many had already surrendered. Quantrill was out of control.

The following year, he was finally arrested. He escaped with big plans to kill President Abraham Lincoln, the Union leader. But soon he decided the troops defending the president were too strong to defeat. Quantrill went back to minor-league raiding. In 1865 Quantrill was captured for good while on a raid in Kentucky. He was shot in a battle with Unionists and died in a military prison.

Quantrill gave up on his plans to kill President Abraham Lincoln *(left)*. But another man shot and killed Lincoln in 1865.

HENRY MCCARTY,
BETTER KNOWN AS BILLY THE KID

Henry McCarty began his life of crime at age sixteen, when he landed in jail for robbing a Chinese laundry. But Henry was sneaky and escaped, possibly by convincing a guard to let him out of his cell. Henry climbed his skinny frame up the chimney and ran.

Henry tried to work as a cowboy. But in that career, his small build was hardly helpful. Soon he turned back to crime. He gambled and hung out with outlaws. It was all pretty harmless until one night in 1877, when he was gambling. A bully started bugging him. A fight broke out. Henry shot the bully in the gut. It took all night for the bully to die. His death made Henry more than just an outlaw. He was a murderer too. He started using a new name, William H. Bonney, which was soon shortened to Billy the Kid.

The Kid fled to New Mexico. He was hired by a man who wanted help defending his ranch and transporting livestock. When other cattle ranchers killed Billy's boss, the Kid joined a new group. He became part of the Regulators, a legal, paid posse charged with seeking revenge.

Unfortunately, when the Regulators caught and killed three men involved in the murder, the governor of New Mexico wasn't pleased. He made legal changes that turned the Regulators into outlaws. The Kid was convicted again. He escaped from jail but didn't get far. A sheriff and his deputies hid out at the home of the Kid's girlfriend. They weren't surprised when the Kid showed up. They were ready—and they shot to kill.

Wanted posters were one of the main ways to track down criminals in the 1800s.

$500 REWARD!
William Bonney
alias BILLY THE KID

This robber and murderer
IS STILL AT LARGE!
I will pay $500 for the capture of Billy the Kid.   by order of

L. WALLACE
May 4th, 1881. Santa Fe, N. Mexico   Gov. New Mexico

SO MANY KIDS
Clearly, Billy the Kid wasn't the only "Kid" of his day. It just so happens "Kid" was a typical nickname for juvenile delinquents during the 1800s.

LAURA BULLION:
THE WILD BUNCH'S DELLA ROSE

When Laura Bullion began her life of crime, she didn't have to look far for role models. She simply followed in the footsteps of both her bank robber dad and her train robber uncle. While still a teen, she joined her uncle as a member of the Wild Bunch, led by Butch Cassidy. Laura knew how to make herself useful. She sold stolen items and passed along stolen money. The gang must have appreciated her efforts. They gave her a nickname: Della Rose.

Laura's Wild Bunch companions *(clockwise from left)* Kid Curry, Bill McCarty, Bill Carver, Ben Kilpatrick, and Tom O'Day pose for a photo in the 1890s.

Riding with train robbers had to be exciting. But it all came to a quick end for Della Rose in 1901. Caught with some stolen money, she was arrested and sentenced to five years in prison. Apparently prison did not agree with her. After her release in 1905, she was a changed woman. It took just one big lie and a major career change to set her life on track.

As a newly freed woman, Della Rose made a new identity for herself. Calling herself Freda Lincoln, she claimed to be a war widow. For the next forty years, she used her sewing skills to support herself as a seamstress, dressmaker, drapery maker, and interior designer.

When she died in 1961, she was around eighty-five years old. Legend has it, Della Rose was the last of the Wild Bunch to go.

WYATT EARP:
COP OR CRIMINAL?

Wyatt Earp was a lawman...sort of. Sure, he was the town constable of Lamar, Missouri, in 1870. But he was also arrested as a horse thief around the same time. And running away to Kansas afterward didn't exactly make him look innocent. For a while, he worked security for businesses in his new town. By 1875 he was back on the police force, this time in Wichita, Kansas.

How was Wyatt as a cop? In a word: *violent*. He was known best for clubbing and fistfighting those who opposed him. In 1876 he was kicked off the Wichita police force. Eh, no biggie. He moved to Dodge City and joined the force there.

The famous gunfight at the O.K. Corral is thought to have lasted only thirty seconds, with about thirty shots fired.

A few years later, though, Wyatt pulled a career-ending stunt. In 1881 he was involved in a gunfight at the O.K. Corral, in Tombstone, Arizona. As an officer of the law, he wasn't charged for the murders he committed there. But the gunfight was more than a matter of law enforcement. It was actually a battle between the Earps and another family they'd been feuding with. After the shootout, the feud continued, and Wyatt kept seeking revenge.

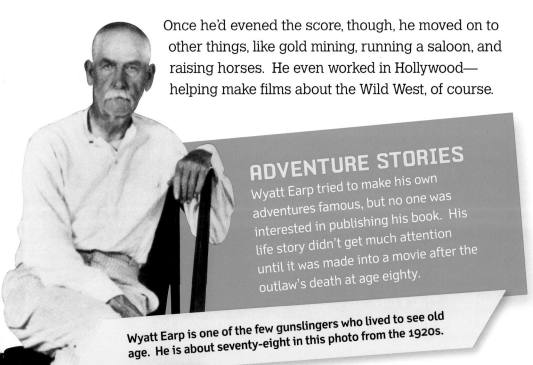

Once he'd evened the score, though, he moved on to other things, like gold mining, running a saloon, and raising horses. He even worked in Hollywood—helping make films about the Wild West, of course.

ADVENTURE STORIES

Wyatt Earp tried to make his own adventures famous, but no one was interested in publishing his book. His life story didn't get much attention until it was made into a movie after the outlaw's death at age eighty.

Wyatt Earp is one of the few gunslingers who lived to see old age. He is about seventy-eight in this photo from the 1920s.

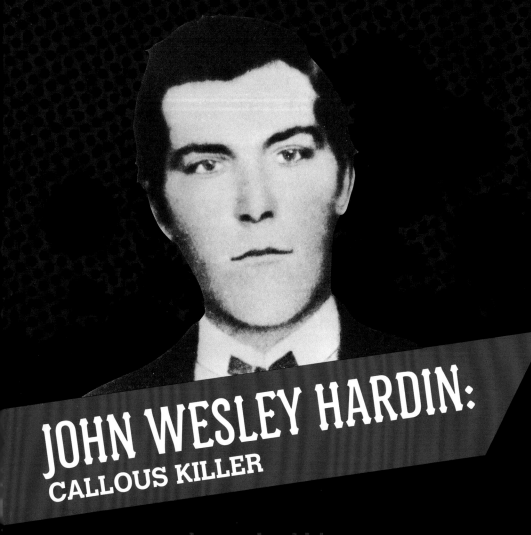

JOHN WESLEY HARDIN: CALLOUS KILLER

John Wesley Hardin always had his reasons for committing his crimes. At fourteen, he stabbed a classmate. But hey, he figured the kid had it coming—he was taunting John. At fifteen, John killed an ex-slave. But according to John, that guy deserved it too. After all, he attacked John after losing a wrestling match. Fleeing from the law and his Texas home, John killed the officials who were after him. Can you blame him, though? He was fighting for his life!

By eighteen, John was working as a cowboy. But he still left dead bodies wherever he went. Was he really so brutal he shot a man for snoring? That's how the story goes, and eventually John claimed he'd killed forty-four men. He was finally arrested for the murder of a deputy sheriff. Found guilty, he spent fifteen years in prison.

Cold-blooded or not, John was no fool. He used his prison time wisely, studying the law. When he was pardoned, he settled into a new career as a lawyer. But this dude just couldn't avoid trouble. Not long after regaining his freedom, John tangled with an El Paso lawman. Some say John hired the lawman to kill someone, and the lawman shot John in the back instead. Others say the lawman killed John just to build his own reputation. Whatever the truth, John lived and died with the attitude of an outlaw.

John supposedly escaped through a hotel window in his longjohns after killing a man for snoring.

R. J. Onderdonk

The Civil War for Fifth Graders
http://www.radford.edu/sbisset/civilwar.htm
The American Civil War riled some outlaws till they were especially vicious. Learn more about it here.

Green, Carl R. *Butch Cassidy.* Berkeley Heights, NJ: Enslow Publishers, 2008. Read this one to learn about Butch and his Wild Bunch.

Harrison, Peter. *The Amazing World of the Wild West.* Leicester, UK: Anness Publishing, 2010. If you want to know about cowboys, outlaws, and Native Americans of the Wild West, this book's for you.

Kerns, Ann. *Was There Really a Gunfight at the O.K. Corral?* Minneapolis: Lerner Publications Company, 2011. Got questions about the famous gun battle involving Wyatt Earp? This book offers answers.

Krohn, Katherine. *Wild West Women.* Minneapolis: Lerner Publications Company, 2006. Want to know more about Belle Starr and other women of the Wild West? Check out this book!

PBS Kids, Wayback, Gold Rush!
http://pbskids.org/wayback/goldrush/index.html
This site has all the info on the gold rush that drew outlaws—and many others—to the West during the mid-1800s.

Roberts, Nancy. *Ghosts of the Wild West.* Columbia: University of South Carolina Press, 2008. Do certain outlaws still haunt the West? Find out by reading this book!

Woog, Adam. *Jesse James.* New York: Chelsea House Publishers, 2010. Get more details about this famous outlaw's life.

Yasuda, Anita. *Explore the Wild West!* White River Junction, VT: Nomad Press, 2012. Try out this book's cool projects, and you'll get to eat, build, and cook like a western outlaw.

INDEX

PHOTO ACKNOWLEDGMENTS

The images in this book are used with the permission of: © 20th Century Fox/The Kobal Collection/Art Resource, NY, pp. 4, 17; © Warner 7 Arts/The Kobal Collection/Art Resource, NY, p. 5; © adoc-photos/CORBIS, p. 6; Library of Congress, pp. 7 (top, LC-USZ62-50007), 7 (bottom, LC-USZ62-007701), 18 (LC-USZ62-132506), 21 (top, LC-USZ62-134452), 21 (bottom, LC-DIG-ppmsca-19470), 24 (LC-DIG-ppmsca-10777); Photo Courtesy of Carbon County Museum © All rights reserved, pp. 8, 9; © American Stock/Archive Photos/Getty Images, pp. 10, 28; © F & A Archive/The Art Archive at Art Resource, NY, p. 11 (top); © Peter Newark's Pictures/The Bridgeman Art Library, pp. 11 (bottom), 20, 26; The Granger Collection, New York, p. 12; © Columbia Pictures/Spyglass/The Kobal Collection/Art Resource, NY, p. 13; © Hulton Archive/Getty Images, p. 14; © iStockphoto.com/Platinus, pp. 15 (background), 23 (background); © Universal History Archive/Getty Images, p. 15 (inset); © Topham/The Image Works, p. 16; © Jonathan S. Blair/National Geographic/Getty Images, p. 19; © Everett Collection/SuperStock, pp. 22, 29; © Interfoto/Alamy, p. 23 (inset); © Adoc-photos/Art Resource, NY, p. 25; © Bowers Museum of Cultural Art/CORBIS, p. 27 (top); © CORBIS, p. 27 (bottom).

Front cover: © John Swartz/American Stock/Archive Photos/Getty Images.

Main body text set in Calvert MT Std Regular 11/16.
Typeface provided by Monotype Typography.